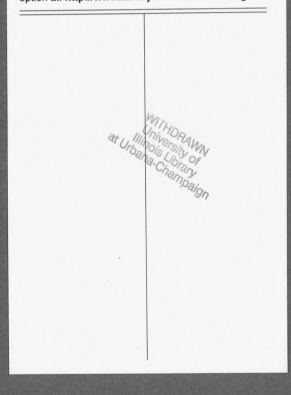

Cairo Inside Out

Cairo Inside Out

Trevor Naylor

**Photographs by
Doriana Dimitrova**

The American University in Cairo Press
Cairo • New York

Page 6 (top, left to right): View from Cairo Tower, Bar of the Windsor Hotel, Bab Zuwayla;
page 6 (bottom, left to right): Hammam of Sultan Inal, Church of St. George, Pool of the Mena House Hotel, Giza;
page 8: The Blue Mosque; page 10: St. George's Bazaar, Old Cairo; page 13: View from Bab Zuwayla.

First published in 2016 by
The American University in Cairo Press
113 Sharia Kasr el Aini, Cairo, Egypt
420 Fifth Avenue, New York, NY 10018
www.aucpress.com

All photographs are by Doriana Dimitrova except for those on pages 72 and 140, which are by Trevor Naylor

Exclusive distribution outside Egypt and North America by I.B.Tauris & Co Ltd., 6 Salem Road, London, W4 2BU

Dar el Kutub No. 14392/15
ISBN 978 977 416 756 0

Dar el Kutub Cataloging-in-Publication Data

Naylor, Trevor
    Cairo Inside Out / Trevor Naylor. —Cairo: The American University in Cairo Press, 2016.
    p.   cm.
    ISBN 978 977 416 756 0
    1.   Cairo (Egypt) Description and Travel
    I.   Dimitrova, Doriana (jt. auth.)
    916.223

1 2 3 4 5   20 19 18 17 16

Designed by Fatiha Bouzidi
Printed in China

This book is dedicated to my wonderful family
and our time together in Egypt

Contents

Acknowledgments

Lots of people helped me write this book and I want to say thank you to all of you, wherever you are.

I want to thank Doriana especially for her photography. I had a clear idea of how I wanted Cairo to look in this very personal book and she took those wishes and improved on them.

Thank you, too, to Narisa Chakrabongse and Miriam Fahmi, who provided invaluable help and advice with my writing and picture organization.

I would also, on behalf of myself and Doriana, wish to thank Mr. Saeed Hefny, who has patiently been our driver and help throughout the making of this book as well as a friend to the Naylor household for seven years.

To everyone at the AUC Press I wish to express my appreciation. To be given the space to make the book I wanted and yet always have the supporting expertise and calm reassurance an author needs makes me a fortunate writer indeed.

Introduction

The idea of this book came to me while I was sitting in the Café Riche in Downtown Cairo.

A long-time regular visitor and occasional denizen of the Egyptian capital, I have learned to anticipate the special late-afternoon moments that seem unique to this great city.

Also, as someone who has spent a lifetime working with books as well as reading them, I wondered if it would be possible to write a book that captured that mood and light.

So the notion of *Cairo Inside Out* was born.

This is not a travel book or guide. It is not a memoir. It is not a history book or a coffee-table book. It attempts to be what Cairo already is: unusual and hard to explain to those who have never been to the city. Why is such a crazy place so alluring? Why do people return to such an overpopulated and polluted city, which regularly drives them nuts?

The answer is: "Because . . ."

How do you capture that concept? That was the question I pondered as I looked out from the quiet of the café onto the noisy street outside and the teeming passersby.

Then it came to me that in the many hours I have spent sitting or wandering around Cairo, most of it is spent inside, looking at the world outside and observing the streets and people as though on a screen.

Books usually portray this city through photography of its most famous buildings and sights from the outside. This is the recognizable Cairo for visitors. But living in and feeling the soul of Cairo is generally an indoor experience, often at the end of a tiring day spent fighting the streets.

Any time you pass from indoors to outdoors or vice versa you have an instant sense of transition. The intensity of the light and heat in Egypt means a great difference in heat or brightness whenever you enter or emerge from somewhere. Such moments, or time spent on one side observing the other, are Cairo at its best.

This book is an attempt to recreate through words and pictures that sense of place and time. Time is a flexible concept in Egypt, and it can be usefully filled by quiet observation of its people and streets. Cairo is an incredibly noisy town, from which you need insulation if you are to recover at the end of the day. Many of the places shown here provide that kind of sanctuary.

This book is by no means a complete look at the city; the selection of places is eclectic but should be familiar to many, while the pictures will bring a far greater feeling of being there than books usually do. Almost a year was spent taking the photographs, with the emphasis always on capturing mood through light and color. This journey only served to convince me more that, although Cairo is often regarded as beige and dusty, it is in fact full of special hues, and the sun is its best friend.

On a personal level, this book began as a way to capture a place I love and occasionally loathe, but never want to abandon. Cairo has for centuries fascinated writers, both local and foreign. Many of those writers were far more capable than I. For me, the challenge was to add a project to that canon that differed from those of its predecessors.

I had not foreseen that the book would evolve into something rather more than an observation of a special place.

We are in the early part of the twenty-first century. The Cairo you see here may well be coming to the end of its time; this conviction grew on me as the photography and writing progressed. *Cairo Inside Out* may become a record of a decade in Cairo's long history when change overcame a place that some people (myself among them) wish could remain the same.

I say this because Cairo, like all cities, is about people.

While writing and taking photographs, Doriana and I enjoyed great kindness and help from the many Cairenes we encountered. In many cases the individuals concerned are Egyptians I proudly count as friends. Often we have known each other for over a quarter of a century and it is they, as much as the place itself, who make a certain business or a particular place so special to visit.

The generation that now lies behind them is not the same as the generation that stands to inherit the rest of the world. It is hard to imagine that they will want to do as their parents did and, in post-revolution Egypt, the future focus is on new cities and technologies, away from the traditional areas of the city that appeal to lovers of history.

This project reminded me that Cairo is not a megacity, but rather an amalgamation of different villages. One can go to the same place twice in twenty years and still be recognized, or pick up a conversation from years before with ease. To be able to catch up on everything you have missed within a few days of returning is also something special to Cairo. Cairenes are very observant and unusually good at remembering people.

Some years ago, Egypt's national football team played a friendly match in Cairo against Australia. With friends from Australia and elsewhere I went to the game, which was fun and exciting. Egypt scored a goal, and during the celebrations the television cameras turned to the crowd supporting Australia. I appeared briefly onscreen. For days after, I was stopped in the street by Egyptians, and even now, more than six years on, I am occasionally stopped with the words "Australia! Football!". Imagine that happening anywhere else.

Rumor and stories abound in Cairo in ways that social media cannot entirely replace. Coffee breaks and other forms of social stimulation provide a platform for news and exchange that is immediate and exciting. To be able to feel a part of that requires ample time spent in a society that appreciates and venerates age.

Sharing such storytelling with Egyptians and local expatriates alike is what underpins life in Cairo. It is also a major part of knowing Cairo inside out.

This book, I hope, reflects how Cairo actually feels. I hope, too, that it evokes good memories for those who already know Cairo, and that it will entice new visitors to this great city.

Trevor Naylor
Cairo, 2016

Nile and Zamalek

For Egypt, the Nile is everything; for the world beyond, it conjures visions of majestically flowing waters bringing new life from the fertile upstream lands to flow past Cairo and into the Mediterranean. Over the centuries it has inspired poets, writers, explorers, and artists.

You would think that the Nile, as huge and constant a presence as it is, would be a simple thing to enjoy day or night. In fact, it most certainly is not, particularly if you want to sit and ponder the river drifting by while reading or enjoying a moment of quiet.

Unlike many urban riverbanks, the edge of the Nile is not made up of public spaces reserved for the people, but rather of areas that are owned, hidden, or simply locked up behind a wall for much of its passage through Cairo. It is certainly usual to see the Nile each day if you are in the city itself, for crossing it is a natural part of one's journey, but getting close is another matter.

In this chapter you will discover how to access the Nile at a variety of points, allowing you to savor its special atmosphere at water level.

Visitors and locals alike are in search of that elusive vista, which could be described as a living painting. Bisected by the river's open, natural flow, the city around it takes on a less frenzied sensibility, and the closer you get to the water the farther from the street you feel. To be on the water is to no longer be in Cairo. To be on the water is somehow to feel connected to the magical land of Egypt as a whole.

It is only natural that a river of such a scale flowing through the heart of the city should make a perfect venue for boats and rowers. The myriad people who live on and beside the Nile only become visible when you are able to access the world they inhabit. In the spirit of seeing the city from the inside out, being near the Nile offers a special and quite separate experience.

A quiet houseboat near Kitkat Square

The Nile is alive all day with craft such as feluccas, racing rowing boats, water taxis, and the occasional police boat or speedboat. That said, in places it is possible to enjoy a few tranquil moments by the vast empty river, and the sense of serenity and agelessness can be almost overwhelming.

The most evocative of all craft are the houseboats moored along parts of the river, especially on the western bank opposite Zamalek. Here is an entirely separate riverine world that one cannot access without invitation.

For westerners, the idea of living aboard a houseboat on the Nile is a romantic ideal that many have enjoyed over the years, although the boats themselves have been moved from time to time, and indeed their very existence has been threatened by officialdom, though it was successfully fought for in recent times.

Houseboats require one to accept that modern comforts can be put aside in the name of a unique opportunity. To live on the Nile and wake by it each day justifies any discomfort, but as the photographs show, it is only the view that gives a

Foyer of a two-
story houseboat

Washing is done in midweek only

Coffee on the water

clue to the houseboats' location. Indeed, the interiors of the boats I have visited reflect the owners' tastes and origins.

Given that so many of the houseboats are occupied by people from western cultures, it can feel as although one is leaving Egypt to sit by the Thames, the Hudson, or the Seine—a nice little break. However, to sit outside on the terrace at water level for breakfast or at sunset is to know you are in Egypt.

The overall impression is hard to absorb at a glance, or to describe in words other than superlatives. Houseboat living for a few years would surely be fun; it could be wonderful if you have a creative career and need daily inspiration or moments of isolation.

Kitkat is the neighborhood to head toward; it is also the eponymous name of a former houseboat that served as a notorious drinking den and drew lovers of a seedy nightlife in the early part of the twentieth century. Today the boats seem more sedate, but behind gates and walls of trees that protect them who knows what goes on? In truth, those I have visited have certainly been more sedate than saucy, despite the seductive alternative lifestyle they offer.

The small procession of wooden houseboats opposite the northern end of Zamalek is the residue of a once-thriving community from a period when they ran the whole length of Cairo. Not only were they home to residents, nightclubs, and casinos; they also harbored wartime espionage in the form of the German spy Johannes Eppler, whose arrest was portrayed in the novel *The Key to Rebecca*. At the center of the scandal was Hekmat Fahmy, the most famous dancer at the Kit Kat Cabaret. She was said to have seduced British officers and extracted information from them, which she passed to Germans who used a houseboat as their base.

In the houseboat shown here, the images covering the walls of the foyer have captured a more modern history, with photography from Egypt's recent revolution. During the early and most intense events of those days, the roads around these houseboats saw the explosive power of a nation at odds with its government.

Looking out across the water today is to experience the serenity and sense of continuity that has held Egypt together for so long. The river's flow is eternal and its passing brings freshness each morning, so much so that the houseboat owners I know seem to start every day anew with great optimism.

Heading upriver to the southern tip of Roda Island is to experience something very different in a place that receives surprisingly few visitors. Again, some effort is needed, but the time spent is well worth it. Here stands the Nilometer, as well as more recent cultural attractions such as the Umm Kulthum Museum.

The Nilometer is a uniquely important spot in Egypt's annual cycle of life for over a thousand years. Here was measured the annual water-level rise (in ells) when the Nile was in flood, in order to predict the fertility of the land and the size of the annual harvest. The country waited for the news, obtained from the measurements, that all would be well. The measurement was also used to compute the annual tax levy payable to the caliph each year in tribute. A rise of between eight and nine meters was cause for joy, and indicates to the modern reader just how vast an area the floodwaters must have covered.

The Nilometer makes an unusual shape in Cairo's skyline

The spectacular roof of the Nilometer

The Umm Kulthum Museum is a small delight

Looking south from Roda Island on an overcast day

The aspect looking south is very different. The gardens around the building allow one to spend time absorbing the sense of place and to imagine how it was, centuries ago, to view the Nile from this unique vantage point. The nearby buildings have a variety of uses, and not all areas are accessible, but there is a spacious terrace that gives an ideal lookout to the river beyond. There is a student art center here, and sometimes work is displayed for sale. During our visit a fashion show was being prepared inside a room that resembled a grand ballroom. Like so many places in Cairo, if you ask politely and show real interest, you will probably be granted access to parallel worlds and meet some friendly Cairenes. This was such a day.

Once inside the Nilometer itself, which has recently been skillfully renovated, the light brings the ornamented walls and ceilings to life. It is a small space, well preserved and simple in construction. The conical, hat-like roof is a modern addition to an edifice that was rebuilt in its current form in 1092 during the Fatimid period, under Caliph al-Mustansir, and is distinct from Cairo's other medieval-period architecture.

A fascinating detour is a visit to the Umm Kulthum Museum, dedicated to the greatest singer in twentieth-century Arab history and showcasing her iconic clothing, from her sunglasses to the dresses she wore to sing her monthly radio broadcasts to an enthralled nation and beyond.

The Nile at dawn, from inside one rowing club looking out onto another

Observing energy and exuberance from the boathouse

Many-layered light at dawn in the rowing clubhouse

The various rowing clubs that sit on the water's edge around Zamalek and Giza are great places to get close to the Nile and see another aspect of the city. Rowing in Egypt is, at its more serious end, dominated by clubs attached to the police, armed forces, and universities. Nevertheless, it is possible to take to the water in a scull at the more public clubs, such as the Egyptian Rowing Club.

All through the year, Egyptians young and old work out by the Nile and run along its corniches, and many get to row. The view of the city from such places, and from the boats, is a treat for the senses. If you are an early riser you will find a whole new world of activity, fun, and breathtaking sunrises that set you up for the day ahead, or for a glorious weekend, in the knowledge that you have done something unusual, healthy, and rather special.

In the process you will be a part of a long, although not continuous, history of the sport, which was a feature of ancient Egypt, when galley rowing was part of regattas held in Luxor. After the pharaonic period, it seems to have fallen into obscurity as a recorded sporting pastime, although the Nile was no doubt just as busy with boats as it is today. During the Second World War, when the British troops stationed in Cairo started building racing boats, interest in the sport was rekindled and, over the next quarter of a century, many boathouses arrived on the banks with their accompanying clubs. As well as the well-known rowing teams from the police, major companies such as the Arab Contractors also founded rowing clubs, followed later by the Cairo University Rowing Club and others.

In the early 1970s Egypt reemerged internationally in the sport, when the Arab Contractors Club participated in the

The water is a real escape despite its closeness to the city

Time for the start

Rowers watched from inside out

Summertime means an early start to beat the heat

Henley Regatta in England, as well as competing in the USA. Soon after, the annual Nile Rowing Festival was launched. Now that Egypt is firmly back on the world rowing stage, the sight of men and women of all ages and backgrounds indulging in a healthy pastime against an amazing backdrop is inspiring. Five Egyptians (three men and two women) qualified for the London Olympics in 2012, indicating the levels achieved in the modern era and the interest and encouragement shown to both sexes.

Some clubs allow visitors to sit by the shore and have a coffee, tea, or even some food if you time your visit well. I have always enjoyed a warm welcome and interesting chats, with a passion for the sport at their heart.

The gentle lapping of water is all you hear as you look inside out from a felucca

Anyone can go out on the Nile for a small charge and experience one of the oldest forms of sailing in the world. Some things in life become a cliché and lose their sense of being special, but sometimes, as with the felucca ride, a cliché is such a thing because it is true. Taking a felucca is a must, and one of the best inside out experiences one can enjoy in all of Egypt.

Offering an ever-changing view, smoothly and quietly moving both with and against the river's flow, the felucca has withstood all technological change through its brilliant simplicity, economy, and (to use a more in-vogue expression) sustainability. Native to Egypt and the Mediterranean since antiquity, these boats offer a wonderful escape for holiday-makers and city dwellers alike.

Whether a planned trip or the result of a moment of exuberance, a felucca ride only varies based on location and companions. In our case, we left from the bank of the Nile close to the Four Seasons Hotel in Garden City. The hour before sundown is the perfect time, and our journey took us close to many of the other places featured in this chapter, as we circled the central fountain in the Nile close to the rowing clubs and the Sofitel, just south of the houseboats.

The quiet, hardworking boatmen must have seen it all in the course of their working lives, and always seem to observe with calm assurance as a sometimes riotous party unfolds before them. Only once have I managed to persuade one (who let his son steer the boat) to join in at charades. Today, of course, these family-run boats usually provide just an hour or an evening's entertainment, unlike the role they played for thousands of years, transporting goods along the Nile Valley.

In Karl Baedeker's 1908 *Guide to Egypt and the Sudan*, he recommends hiring such boats, which are used for the transportation of sugarcane, cotton, and other goods, and adds: "No luxury of course, must be looked for, but its absence is compensated by the close relations with the land and people, into which the traveler is brought." He also notes that "a young attendant with some knowledge of cooking may be obtained for £E 2 to 3 per month [less that one dollar these days] who will also do the necessary marketing in the villages." It is easy to imagine the felucca captains of today being part of a family line that steered such travelers and goods in times long gone.

With the sunset, the light changing from gold to orange, and the sense of quiet accompanied by the breeze of movement, a felucca trip at day's end should soothe the soul of any traveler. Let go and absorb the atmosphere of the Nile and the gentle swirl of the water.

Photographs can capture a great deal, such as the changing light on the water, but try to hang on to the feeling of deep calm and tranquility imparted by a felucca trip and keep the memory as a protection against the hustle and bustle of the modern city. In Upper Egypt you can hire such craft to sleep on and move from place to place under cloudless skies, both day and night—an opportunity to be seized.

Another, separate community takes refuge between the Corniche and the river

Stylish decoration and cooling
architecture are hallmarks of
good hotel design

This window offers an
astonishing panorama and
a cool place to hide

Looking out from the Gezira Sofitel the next stop is Aswan, in the mind's eye at least

Now we return to the southern tip of Gezira Island and one of the most spectacular hotel settings. The Sofitel, formerly the Sheraton El Gezirah, is a circular hotel with views in all directions. Looking at this opulence today it must come as a surprise to learn that this island only emerged and separated fully from mud banks in the nineteenth century. It was in fact only stabilized as a place to inhabit after the opening of the first Aswan Dam. The southern half of the island (the northern end being Zamalek) was later laid out by the British, who had been granted access by Khedive Tawfiq.

A visit to this luxurious hotel in its ideal setting is a real treat. After struggling in the traffic or working hard at sight-seeing, a drink inside or outside offers a well-earned moment of self-indulgence.

This hotel is in as central a place in Cairo as you can get. Lying in the middle of the river, in the heart of the city, and at water level, its unsurpassed view is a sight to behold when you need to get away, or to really celebrate. An hour or more spent gazing out from within the hotel or its gardens will both recharge your batteries and remind you of the space

The Sofitel lobby is a fine spot to plan
your next outdoor venture

Cairo fills. Looking around at the combination of buildings, sky, and water truly gives a sense of the vastness of the space around you.

Many places touch the Nile, but few allow quiet time or space around oneself. The Nile is Cairo's heartbeat and Egypt's unique life force. Sitting by it always raises the spirits and stimulates conversation among friends. Whether you see it from inside or out, the Nile refreshes you. More often than not the sight will be from a car or taxi; perhaps from a home or while coming in to land from elsewhere. Whenever and wherever you glimpse it, the sight is magical, as if the mighty river is telling you, "I am here."

Zamalek's northern tip has one of the most idyllic spots in Cairo from which to look inside out—Sequoia restaurant

Across the water from the houseboats, at the very northern tip of Zamalek, is a complex of restaurants open from early morning until deep into the night, with Sequoia at the center of this delightful corner. With views north to the Imbaba Bridge and with the east and west banks of the Nile far enough away to allow one to appreciate the quiet calm of the river at one of its widest points within the city, this is an island within an island.

Sitting here, it's surprising to reflect that less than one hundred years ago, this was a spot reached by ferry from the Bulaq area to the east, then the city's river harbor and a key transport hub linking the economy of the Delta with markets in Upper Egypt and Cairo. Zamalek's art deco blossoming was just beginning, as the northern end of Gezira Island was bought for development and divided into plots for resale in 1905–1907.

While the buildings that arose are nowadays seen as marvels of period architecture and create a unique atmosphere in which to wander, the development saw the end of Gezira as an island of green beauty. However, to sit in Sequoia now and imagine what modern developers would have done is to be thankful for the mostly French and Italian architects who planned something rather lovely.

As you can see from the photographs, the setting of this restaurant is truly delightful at sunset, and is a place to enjoy a unique sense of people and place, as the well-heeled local clientele make this a lively spot late into the night. For much of the day, however, or during midweek, it can also be a haven for those who seek some quiet to read or think. The river traffic of working and pleasure craft is a reminder that one is in the midst of a busy place; Cairo is a megacity.

Should you walk around the roads that lead to Sequoia you will find that, buried behind gates and (generally) friendly security guards, there are ways to access the riverbank. With coffee shops, wedding boats, plant nurseries, rowing clubs, and mosques sitting cheek by jowl along the edge, you can, with a little effort, see more of the Nile.

Sequoia has an amazing setting but people bring it alive

The grounds of the Cairo Opera House
provide a welcome shaded walk

The El Sawy Culture Wheel is an oasis looking out
onto the cramped towers of Zamalek beyond

The place to really get close to the river is the El Sawy Culture Wheel, situated beneath the busiest bridge crossing the island and spread across an area that was once a garbage tip and no-go area. Muhammad El Sawy opened the cultural center in 2003 and dedicated it to his father, Abdel Moneim El Sawy, author of a string of novels with the series title *The Wheel*.

Now an established part of Cairo's cultural life and a real oasis for people of all ages, the Culture Wheel plays a major role in encouraging artistic expression and provides a venue for both new and established artists and musicians.

It is also one of the rare places in Cairo that anyone can enter freely and sit quietly to work, watch the river, read, and relax. With an atmosphere designed to encourage equality and cultural understanding, it offers a sense of quiet self-confidence.

The various areas allow you to sit and observe Cairo from different angles, but the overall feeling of being in what is almost another city altogether allows escape from the hubbub just beyond the gates or the river Nile. The light at day's end and at night can be magical. For an even greater sense of escape, you can take the water taxi from under the bridge.

The Culture Wheel is both an indoor and outdoor experience, but most of the greatest secrets of Cairo's architectural past lie inside the residential buildings of Zamalek.

The El Sawy Culture Wheel lies under a bridge

Recent attempts to brighten up the city with splashes
of color help lift the spirits

Looking up can bring rewards even
as you climb the stairs

I obviously cannot encourage the reader to wander into other people's homes and buildings uninvited, which is a pity because, as anyone who has ever strolled around Zamalek knows, it is the most tempting of places for those who love interior style and design.

The beguiling glimpses into the foyers of the buildings on either side of 26th July Street are part of the mostly expat syndrome I call "see beyond the *bawwab* (doorman)." All buildings have a guardian of some kind, although in the new century the quality of security and general standards of cleanliness seem to have fallen away. In times past, being the front man for a building was a role to be admired and a job done with pride.

While I would never advocate illegally entering anywhere, there are many buildings that have some business role to play, such as hotels, restaurants, bars, cafés, and bookstores, which means you can legitimately enter them and wander (or wonder) around them. All of the pictures in this part of the book are in such buildings, and provide a window onto the inside out world of Cairo. The coolness and quiet that immediately envelop you as you move indoors is clear in these evocative photographs. It is easy to speak of the city's faded glory, but that fails to acknowledge its inescapably cyclical

nature. All these places have seen good times and bad, and will do so again. One thing which is certain is that in Egypt as much as anywhere else the value of property equates with family wealth and security and such beautiful buildings are, at least inside, safe from complete decay.

Foyers, windows, elevators, and stairs reveal a time about a century ago when great care and attention to detail prevailed and the creation of a wonderful building to compete with its neighbors involved excellent workmanship. If you are fortunate enough to be invited into homes in Zamalek, accept the offer with alacrity. The views can be breathtaking.

This tiny selection of pictures gives some indication of how Zamalek at ground level is repurposed so well. Here we have hotels and art galleries, stores and bookstore cafés, and the neighborhood is nirvana for those with a staircase or elevator fetish.

The building back views do not provide the same inspiration for students of architecture or life, as they often reveal the waste end of a living building and rather detract from the romantic sensation of being in another century, or indeed in Paris.

With a camera, a smile, and a smattering of Arabic you can persuade the *bawwab* to let you wander around a little in most buildings, but don't push your luck.

Life beyond the doormen in Zamalek is exciting

FOLLOWING PAGES:
The astonishingly beautiful Mayfair Hotel

Les Livres de France bookstore is on the first floor of
17 Brazil Street and blends well with the world outside

Heritage and modernity in the Zamalek
Art Gallery's perfectly lit foyer

The elegance of this stairway in the building of
the Longchamps Hotel leads the imagination
back nearly a century

Behind most buildings you will find
the rawness of Cairo's backstreets

True symmetry is rare but the Mayfair Hotel's lobby
comes close to achieving it

Zamalek has reinvented itself in some buildings with elegant stores and bric-a-brac emporia. Great for browsing.

Cool light and bright colors just off Brazil and 26th July streets

The building hosting the Loft Gallery and Sufi Bookstore and Café is a delight

Zamalek's Sufi Bookstore and Café
is a haven for students, away from
the babble of the world outside

The glass door of Diwan Bookstore is a window
familiar to all Zamalek book lovers

Zamalek's Hotel Longchamps provides
a small cocoon for those who wish to
enjoy a quiet afternoon tea

The wonderful stairwell in the building
of the Hotel Longchamps

For a family outing or romantic experience the viewing gallery
of the Cairo Tower is unrivaled and breathtaking

There is a tradition in architecture that continues today of building tall, tower-like buildings in major cities across the globe. Usually commissioned by men wishing to make a mark on both the present and posterity, they often still dominate the skylines of their cities today. The Cairo Tower is Egypt's version of this phenomenon and is, by world standards, one of the more attractively designed and eye-catching examples of its kind. Like the pyramids and other such members of the tall-building club, size matters, and the scale of this tower is impressive.

Built in 1961 and inaugurated by Gamal Abdel Nasser, with a recent and successful refurbishment that has added changing light effects at night, the Cairo Tower is well worth a visit. At 187 meters tall it is a long elevator ride to the top . . .

or some 2,500 steps, if you wish to stretch your legs. At the top are restaurants and the viewing gallery. As with many of Cairo's more elevated landmarks there is a certain element of luck to this, but the view on a clear day does take one's breath away.

To see all across Cairo to the Pyramids and the Citadel, and to see the Nile winding far to the north explains the geography of the city better than any map. You can spend a long time working out where all the places you know on the ground actually are. Often the gallery is full of young local couples and families enjoying the breeze and taking photographs. It's a carefree spot and whether you are inside the restaurant or outside it, the tower provides the best high-rise view of Cairo you can find.

Zamalek's famous Cairo Tower provides a 360-degree panorama,
but why not look down as well?

Downtown Cairo

With variety and sheer modern grandeur, Downtown Cairo manages to retain a separate personality from the rest of the city.

This sense of age and prestige stems from its unique mix of architectural styles and the area's distinctive position as a crossing point for all the major events of Egypt's recent history.

These days it requires no small feat of the imagination to see the center of Cairo as it was when Khedive Ismail's nineteenth-century dream of a "Paris by the Nile" became a reality. He had returned to Cairo after a visit to Paris in 1867 for the Exposition Universelle, where Egypt's pavilion had been a huge success in presenting ancient Egypt and the Orient as the next exciting travel destination of the time.

The khedive, however, was more interested in bringing Europe to Egypt, and set about developing a downtown district that imitated the quarters of Paris in style and design.

Today there remain enough major streets and statues to evoke a European-style city, although daily life has clearly imparted Downtown with a distinctly Egyptian flavor.

According to Baedeker's Egypt guidebook of 1908, the khedive offered sites in the area from Azbakiya and Abdin Palace westward to the Nile to "anyone who would undertake to build on each a house worth at least 30,000 francs within eighteen months." This suggests the khedive was in a hurry to get his Paris-style Cairo on the move. Baedeker's writers of the day seemed unimpressed, commenting that "most of the houses are architecturally uninteresting."

However, there are lots of interesting interiors to explore, which can be done over the course of a one- or two-day slow wander through the places chosen here—if you pace your journey and look beyond the crowds and noisy traffic.

A good place to begin is also an easy place to find. The American University in Cairo (AUC) these days runs most of its classes on its vast campus in New Cairo, but its original,

The American University in Cairo's beautifully decorated Oriental Hall (above) and staircase (opposite)

well-preserved building sits proudly on the edge of Tahrir Square and has been witness to many of Egypt's most volatile and moving events of the last one hundred years.

Once you are on campus, you can choose to sit either inside or out, for it has some of the prettiest gardens for miles around and offers a shady place to relax, read, and plan one's walk. It is also a good starting point if you wish to visit the AUC Bookstore, which offers a wide range of books on Egypt in English and other languages with which to accompany your visit.

The buildings comprising the original campus include some very attractive neo-Islamic architecture, which has been lovingly maintained and is well worth a visit if you can find your way around. The main building facing Tahrir Square has an elegant foyer and staircase, which offers a cool interior lit by stained glass and exquisite geometric designs. This, the Khairy Pasha Palace, was built in the 1860s by the then Egyptian minister of education, Khairy Pasha, as part of the early development of the new Downtown Cairo district.

Beyond the walls of the American University in Cairo campus lie busy intersections and noise

The building was acquired by Charles Watson, AUC's founding president, in 1919, and shortly after opened as the original structure of AUC, dedicated to being an educational center for the cultural enrichment and modernization of Egypt.

One room that will take your breath away is the recently restored Oriental Hall, situated by the fountain courtyard at AUC. While not open to the public all the time, it is usually accessible during working hours. Every inch of this small space is decorated to the highest standards. As a platform for speakers and events, it has hosted many of the talks and conversations that have helped make AUC such a key component of Egypt's cultural and educational development over the past century.

Looking across the lush gardens, you can see the vast expanse of Midan Tahrir, overshadowed by the gloomy, brutalist Mugamma building. This vast government office block is best viewed from as far away as possible.

Setting out for Downtown thankfully takes you away from Tahrir along the nearby Talaat Harb Street. Here a quick visit to the Oum El Dounia gift shop and bookstore allows for a more elevated view of the area from their terrace. Of course, one may travel back in one's mind as far as one's historical knowledge permits, but for me it is hard to be in such vantage points and not recall the days of Egypt's 2011 revolution.

The formidable Mugamma is Egypt's great testament to 1940s modernist architecture, also synonymous with unending bureaucratic procedures

The sweeping view on a clear day from the Oum El Dounia store on Talaat Harb Street

Beyond the basic drinks menu, the Horreya offers customers a great shoeshine with a smile

The 'dry' end of the Horreya Bar looks out over Bab al-Luq and a constant movement of people and cars

Beguiling and historically fascinating Stella beer graphics

Nearby, in Bab al-Luq, is a high spot that exemplifies the inside out experience and remains a cherished haunt for many foreign visitors.

The Horreya Bar has many facets, which create a sense of either enjoyment or expectation, along with some occasional low-level anxiety. Having been a visitor on many occasions across some thirty years, my enjoyment of this unique space and atmosphere depends entirely on the context of my visit that day or evening.

On those occasions where the nearby streets are simply too loud or crowded, Horreya offers a sanctuary (although not a cool one on hot days, as there is no air-conditioning). A cool drink and a shoeshine make a winning combination, along with the chance to watch the world go by and speculate on the

The mirrors afford great opportunities for discreet people-watching

lives of the others sharing your sense of escapism. Horreya is a split universe, with floor-level windows for the no-alcohol end and, these days, a darker end with the light cut out for those enjoying Egypt's finest beers. The light that moves through the room over the day picks out every detail in this spot, which, despite its recent renovation, has already reverted to its one-star shabbiness. The reflections of the surrounding street and its conservative people, which appear in the Stella Beer mirrors, highlight the contradictory attitudes to drinking in Egypt.

The only anxiety that might accompany a trip to the Horreya is whether, having arranged to meet someone there,

it will be open. There are many different national holidays in Cairo, based around religion as well as famous military and historic events, but exactly which ones mean the bars will close is still a mystery.

Sharing this place with someone for the first time is always a fun experience. In the evening, the inside out feeling turns outside in as the lights come on and cast their glow across the pavement, turning Horreya into a welcoming spot as you step into the light for a drink or some powerful coffee. After one visit, your order will be permanently logged in a waiter's mind, and repeated until you say no.

The Windsor Hotel Barrel Bar has a magnificent stillness that allows you to enjoy its many details

In truth, few people see more of this old hotel than its public areas of foyer and bar, but despite this its atmosphere is strong enough to leave a mark in the memories of all visitors. One day this will surely change, as all things must. A fresh broom will brush away the cobwebs, and take away the Windsor's charm as well. Until that day comes, though, enjoy this special space and talk to its staff, who are a living history.

The Windsor was not purpose-built as a hotel; it was a bathhouse for the Egyptian royal family at the end of the nineteenth century before serving as a British officers' club for many years. Eventually it was purchased by a Swiss hotelier as an annex to the famous (now destroyed) Shepheard's Hotel in the nearby Azbakiya Gardens, and operated as the Hotel Windsor–Maison Suisse.

The period feel one enjoys today in the famous barrel bar and breakfast room are as close as you can get to being in authentic colonial Cairo, and the possibility that you might find yourself sharing a meal or drink with the family owners is a refreshing change from corporate hotel management. However, if you expect speedy service, lightning-fast Wi-Fi, and a latte, then you should skip this treat.

The key to the Windsor is its silence. The seats by the windows allow you to read or ruminate while enjoying a private view of the streets outside. Depending on which side of the room you are on, the view is a coffee house, a junction, or a street of food vendors, all busy with people who don't look up. From your secluded perch, you can sit and simply observe life. This is a soothing way to pass the time of day and ponder the glorious, ever-changing light.

Before leaving, don't forget to study the framed posters and reviews around the walls, including one from their most famous recent traveler, Michael Palin, who stayed here as he went around the world in eighty days (and came back to the Windsor again, as he loved the place).

The atmosphere of spaces such as this defy photography, so make sure you allow time for the feelings to seep into your memory.

Later evening shows the bar at its cosmopolitan best. The interaction of foreign visitors and Egyptians makes for a noisy mix and has done much over the years to encourage friendships and understanding. Opinions are not sought; they are expected. Once inside the Horreya, it is unlikely you will get out that quickly.

If you're seeking a more sedate late-afternoon experience to wind down the day, you could do no better than visit one of the world's greatest time capsules on Alfi Bey Street just off 26th July Street downtown.

One of the challenges of writing any book about Cairo is finding new things to say about its landmarks and wonderful people. The Windsor is a test on both counts.

Window light in the Windsor's Barrel Bar

The breakfast room of the Windsor Hotel transports you to another time and place while you enjoy the quality of its light

The décor of the Windsor's Barrel Bar has evolved
in its own special way over many years

The Windsor elevator shaft casts light
through the center of the whole building

Leaving the Windsor's front door plunges you
straight back into the city's animated street life

The Café Riche is situated on Talaat Harb Street and is one of the iconic spots to visit in Downtown Cairo. Whether your interests incline toward politics, art, literature, or modern history, this café has something to offer. Its atmosphere is unique and its view onto the street from the quiet calm of a historic interior provides a window onto modern Egypt, where epoch-making moments took place.

The seemingly unchanging decor, staff, and food and beverage offerings create an experience to be savored at least once (or, in my case, a hundred times). The walls are adorned with photographs and artworks depicting Egypt's most famous writers, musicians, and artists, as well as art devoted to Nobel laureate Naguib Mahfouz.

Café Riche is where journalists head to write or read, talk and drink, and catch up on news. It was this space and this view of the world outside that inspired this book. Regular visits create a connection with the past that provides an anchor in the constantly changing atmosphere of the region today.

A landmark of Downtown Cairo since it opened in 1908, numerous stories of intrigue surround the Café Riche. The 1952 plot by Gamal Abdel Nasser and the Free Officers was hatched and initiated from the Riche. In the 2011 revolution, the café was an ideal distance from everything that was happening in Tahrir Square and managed, perhaps because of its respected place in Cairene history, to survive even when fighting and chaos swirled around it.

Other memorable moments include live performances by Umm Kulthum, hosting King Farouk as a customer, and having the novel *Karnak Café* set in its four walls by Naguib Mahfouz. The memory of incidents such as these still inhabits the fabric of the Café Riche, and if you sit awhile you can bring them to life.

The Café Riche wears its Egyptian
identity with pride

From the café's soothing dark interior you can watch
the world go by on Talaat Harb Street

In addition to food and drink, Downtown offers another cultural treat, one that is rapidly disappearing elsewhere in the world—the old-fashioned bookshop.

Wandering around the streets of Downtown it is still possible to understand why Khedive Ismail wanted this area to emulate Paris and commissioned French architects to bring that sophisticated European feel to nineteenth-century Cairo. His dream was the rapid development of Egypt, and to achieve that he chose to follow what he saw as the best in the world at that time. No surprise then that, with such beautiful buildings and rich denizens, many bookstores opened in the area. A number remain, but few offer the wide range of European languages once available. When I first arrived in Cairo to sell books myself, I was impressed by the quality of the bookstores, but the tailing off of quality stores owned by genuinely expert booksellers is one of the reasons Downtown is losing its cultural appeal to the European traveler.

Leaving the Café Riche takes you out of the 1950s to the noisy present day

The café's graphic style is seen here inside out and back to front

Sobhy Greiss (left), born in 1901, opened the Anglo-Egyptian Bookstore in 1928; his son, Amir Greiss (right), then ran the store after him. Amir's sons are now in charge

How many modern-day readers remember the Loeb Classical Library?

A wrought-iron staircase uses minimum space, as books are king in the Anglo-Egyptian Bookshop

In the heart of Downtown, the Anglo-Egyptian Bookshop has been a source of fine books for three generations

A walk to Muhammad Farid Street can include several old bookstores, including the famed Lehnert and Landrock on Sherif Street and Reader's Corner on Abdel Khaliq Tharwat Street (which now offers framing services).

The Anglo-Egyptian Bookshop has been a center of academic and educational bookselling for three generations. Here is a place to browse for unexpected delights. The Greiss family tradition of building a stock of books and showing patience in selling them is refreshing in the fast-moving retail world of the twenty-first century. The high ceilings and tall bookshelves come complete with well-informed assistance from loyal and intelligent bookstore staff. The cool interior is just a window away from the hectic road, and this lookout (especially if you are offered tea or coffee) is a great little stop on your journey around Cairo's modern heart.

The hum of business and the solid reliability of this bookstore's library atmosphere makes for another place where you can relax and sense the whiff of history. Certainly it's clear when looking around the Anglo-Egyptian Bookstore that the previous generations have created a place that moves forward with publishing changes, but the bookstore is resolute in the standards of its service and its welcoming of customers, old and new.

The real world as seen from the Fontana Hotel disco

The Fontana's bar is simple but functional

You may have seen the flags of the Fontana as you drive along the Sixth of October Bridge. Next time make a visit.

A more offbeat place, and one that offers an unparalleled view, takes you out of Downtown toward Ramses Square, which for sheer numbers of people and traffic is surely one of the noisiest and most ghastly places one can imagine.

However, if you head upward to seek an aerial perspective of this huge circle of life, you may come across surprises like the Hotel Fontana. A little-known upper-floor hotel, the Fontana has been perched above Ramses Square for many years, offering a fine view, a cool bar and disco, and food. Its panoramic lookout can often be enjoyed in solitary comfort following the post-revolution decline in tourism, and the service is quietly efficient.

Ramses Square was the home of the giant statue of Ramesses II from 1955 until 2006, when it was transported for restoration to a spot near its new (future) home in the Grand Egyptian Museum. Prior to its arrival in the square, this area was called Bab al-Hadid Square, and in the late nineteenth century was designated as the northern gate to the modern city in Khedive Ismail's downtown plan.

Despite the departure of the statue, the presence of Ramses Railway Station, taking up one whole side of the square, means the name remains relevant today.

As with so many things in modern Cairo, one must look beyond the sometimes ugly present to see beauty and feel the past. From the Fontana you can find time and space to do that. Again, a key element of your contemplation will be the changing effect of the sunlight and skies on the scene surveyed.

HERE AND OVERLEAF: The views from the Fontana Hotel in Ramses Square

Eating is a significant part of daily life in Egypt, and countless restaurants and fast-food venues line Cairo's myriad streets and alleyways. Some are beloved by Egyptians and some are well known to visitors. Outside of hotels, however, there are few places where Egyptian cuisine can be genuinely enjoyed by both. Felfela has been one such place since 1959.

Felfela's somewhat crazy interior design is a true delight. Careful examination of walls and ceilings show it to be a half-open-air restaurant that could only survive in a hot,

dry country. The food and service are great value, both for the quality of meals and the opportunity to sit and watch a restaurant at work. All around you is evidence of famous past visitors and of busier tourist times.

The pictures shared here show the harsh daylight being suffused into cool, almost church-like colors, which help create a soothing atmosphere. Felfela can be enjoyed at any time of day. The food from their grill is excellent, and some

Felfela restaurant is a tourist trap worth falling into

Felfela restaurant, off Talaat Harb Street,
hosts an eclectic range of decorative objects

dishes, such as shakshuka and Dawood Pasha, you will not find readily elsewhere.

After this, a short walk to Talaat Harb Square and Groppi may provide a finish to your day or start to your evening.

This busy circle in the center of multiple streets hosts a statue of Talaat Harb, a leading Egyptian economist and key figure in his country's economic and financial life in the early part of the twentieth century. He stands surrounded by a ring of recently renovated buildings that boast a heterogeneous

mix of architectural styles, which is part of what makes Downtown so special. When viewed from Groppi, the famous confectioner's store, it is indeed a grand sight.

Groppi was a global brand till the end of the 1950s, and their chocolate creations were world renowned. Their tearoom was *the* place to be seen, and foreign royalty frequently paid a visit. Now it is none of these things, but the place retains an unmistakable allure.

Five minutes' navigation north from the square you will find another offbeat rooftop well worth a visit. The Odeon Hotel is not frequented for its beauty or style, but it does have a fine, if gritty, view of the backstreets of this area. While not a transport of delight, it brings one close to a different reality. Furthermore, once you are in its elevator your only thought will be the hope that you emerge again to somewhere better.

The roof of the Odeon Hotel has a hideway café
and a view of Downtown's back alleys

This view from Groppi's doorway presents
a triptych though which Downtown Cairo
today and in the past may be viewed

City Gates to the Muqattam Hills

Now we will attempt some serious time travel, for this chapter is a wander through medieval Cairo, which is still largely intact today.

This journey starts by the Khan al-Khalili bazaar and takes us south and east to the City of the Dead and the Citadel before we arrive above Cairo at the Muqattam Hills. Medieval Cairo is an intensely cramped area of narrow streets and historic buildings that fill the space between the modern highways of al-Geish and Salah Salem streets, an intense visual and aural experience for any visitor.

There are few places I know of in the world where you can be such an obvious outsider and yet so happily absorbed by a place, which carries on with its daily business as you pass through. The streets of this area are packed with people, animals, cars, and shops, which coexist in an economic cocoon that its population rarely leaves, as almost all its requirements are locally met.

In fiction, time travel involves an instantaneous transition from one place and time to another, to the future, the past, or perhaps a parallel universe. In medieval Cairo, this change occurs as you pass between the magnificent buildings that comprise the Sultan al-Ghuri Complex, with the mosque–madrasa on one side, and the mausoleum and *sabil-kuttab* (a public water facility and Qur'anic school) on the other.

These two edifices stand guard at one entry to Mu'izz li-Din Illah Street and the crushingly busy and exciting path toward Bab Zuwayla, Fatimid Cairo's southern gate, one of just three remaining of the city's many historic entry points.

Some will arrive and, looking from the main street into the past, so close and yet so daunting, will wonder if going on makes sense.

In fact there is a choice—to enter what looks like a maelstrom of humanity with no room for yet more people, or to

Beyond the mausoleum of Sultan al-Ghuri lies the path to Bab Zuwayla (opposite) and the Street of the Tentmakers

head instead to the calmer side of al-Azhar Street and the easy shopping of Khan al-Khalili. Ignore that less-fulfilling option.

The short walk to the actual gate of Bab Zuwayla is absorbing and sets the tone for the places you may choose

Bab Zuwayla's twin minarets are a steep winding climb, which one often shares with other visitors

The play of light as you move around is delightful

Looking down you can see the mosque of al-Salih Tala'i' and the roof of the Street of the Tentmakers

to visit in the area. The juxtaposition of the man claiming to be Cairo's only remaining fez maker and the store opposite, selling gaudy new underwear and lurid belly-dancing out-fits, is one of those moments when you are caught between past and present.

There are innumerable buildings and places to see or stop at in this complex area, and the examples I can give only scratch the surface. Soon the tall, powerful minarets of Bab

The enormous mosque of al-Muʾayyad stands next to Bab Zuwayla

Zuwayla loom before you and you arrive at what feels like a gateway to history.

This gate, built in 1092, is important architecturally as an example of work by the Fatimids, who brought with them the techniques of stone masonry for building the new city walls and gates. The Fatimids invaded Egypt from Tunisia and founded what we now call Cairo (al-Qahira—the Victorious) in AD 969. Over the next two hundred years they introduced a North African influence in mosque design, before their overthrow by the great warrior Saladin and the beginning of the Ayyubid dynasty.

From these twin towers you have one of the great inside outs of Cairo. The steep climb inside them is the precursor to a wonderful moment when you emerge at the top and look around in all directions over the oldest part of Cairo and the evidence of its long history.

Bab Zuwayla is a popular spot with Egyptians and visitors alike, and a good place to take and share pictures and your experience with those around you. The panoramic view provides a good chance for orientation. Below the gate is the mosque of al-Muʾayyad, which forms part of the same complex and was completed around 1420.

The view down on such edifices shows the scale of these early architectural undertakings. Set against the surrounding streets and the modern, often shoddily built, housing, these enormous monuments still dominate and exude a sense of power and security.

The cool light of the tentmakers' stalls and their warm welcome makes the Street of the Tentmakers a special place

Bargain hard as you know you will only have a partial victory whatever you do

Looking south from the gate you can follow the rooftop of the Street of the Tentmakers in anticipation of your next stopping point. To the left is another square building and courtyard, which is the mosque of al-Salih Tala'i'.

On your descent back to street level, allow yourself to drift back in time, although not all the thoughts may be romantic oriental visions. True, this gate was the starting point for the caravans to Mecca and the south, but it was also the site for executions of various forms. In the sixteenth century it must have been a place to visit with one eye on an escape route, as it was associated with all manner of street life and the false hopes offered by miracle healers.

At ground level you pass through the gates themselves and are assailed by sights and sounds from all directions, although by now your thoughts may be running to a drink of tea in a cool place. The near end of Shari' al-Khayamiya, or the Street of the Tentmakers, beckons ahead.

As you pass the mosque of al-Salih Tala'i' (built in 1160) on your left, it is worth remembering that, despite being

an important figure of the time and a vizier, the mosque's founder, al-Malik al-Salih Tala'i' could not escape the intrigues of the era, the memories of which make walking around this area today so exciting. Poisoned by a princess, he still managed to arrange for her death before he breathed his last.

The Street of the Tentmakers was built in 1650 and is the only extant covered market street left in medieval Cairo. Its aim then was to provide the tents, cloths, and saddles for those setting out on the pilgrimage to Mecca in the great caravans of the day. It has remained largely unchanged, and indeed is populated by families who in some cases can trace their heritage of appliqué making back over almost four centuries.

Refreshingly cooler than Mu'izz Street, and illuminated with diffused sunlight, the Street of the Tentmakers is a welcome break from the streets around it. While its expert craftspeople continue to make goods to order, their mainstay is the output of appliqué quilts and bags destined for the tourist market.

The Street of the Tentmakers remains a working and trading center
which makes visiting and observing most exciting

Inside the main gate of Ibn Tulun Mosque

From inside Ibn Tulun Mosque you can see
Cairo through every space of wall and gate

The prayer areas of Ibn Tulun exude quiet
reverence on a monumental scale

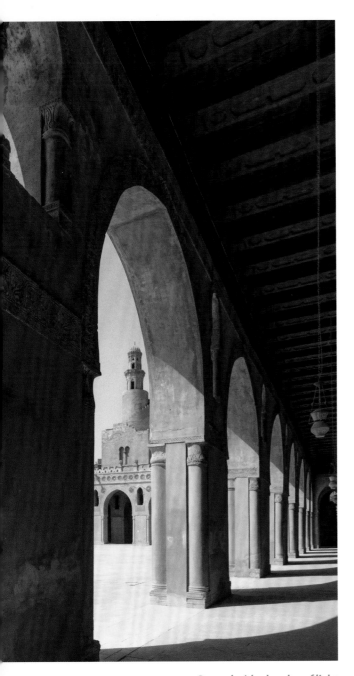

If you have been given a rough time by hawkers in the Khan al-Khalili or at the pyramids, the soft sell with tea or lemon juice here is a delight. If you relax and go with it, a highly enjoyable conversation may ensue. Furthermore, you will find out that everyone here really does know the craft they have been trained in.

Looking out from any of the small stalls while sitting on a bench is a delight. Passing you are hardworking folk making deliveries or shopping, as they have for hundreds of years. It is difficult to take a bad photograph here.

Wherever you look, there is a view worth savoring. The subtle ambience of these few hundred meters is exceptional, and will call you back each time you visit Cairo.

What is the greatest building to visit in Cairo? This is a question with no correct answer. However, the mosque of Ibn Tulun would top many lists. It is certainly my favorite, and indeed I would argue that, with its simple elegance and geometry, Ibn Tulun is one of the world's great architectural secrets. Long may it stay that way, so it can be enjoyed for its relative quiet and the sense of peaceful strength it conveys.

Ibn Tulun is also the ideal spot for a wide variety of inside out experiences. Its layers of courtyards and doorways, arches and crenellations, and unique (in Egypt) minaret all provide delightful places from which to look out on the passing world. When work began in 876 on this massive Friday mosque, no one could have foreseen that, just over a thousand years later, this space would be surrounded on all sides by high-rise apartment blocks with roof dwellers and satellite dishes as far as the eye can see. The roads around the mosque are an area of extreme human density, and the sudden sense of quiet and emptiness when you enter the mosque is disarming.

Ahmad Ibn Tulun was sent to Egypt from Baghdad in 868. By the time he began building this great mosque, he had moved from being governor of Fustat to being the first ruler of an independent Egypt since Cleopatra. By refusing to pay tribute to the Abbasid caliph he effectively proclaimed himself the founder of a new dynasty.

Between the inner and outer walls of Ibn Tulun is a wide area
of extra defense and architectual variety

The mosque is a glory to explore alone or with friends. It is
a place where you can sit all day and read, or do nothing but
revel in the silence. It is a space that inspires creative thinking
and meditation.

It is also a place to look out from and marvel.

All around, as far as the eye can see, are minarets and
modern skylines. The mosque itself covers over six acres and
was intended to host Friday prayers for the entire area in one
place. That must have been quite a sight.

The mosque of Ibn Tulun will deliver a wonderful experience, something hard to guarantee when recommending most
excursions. It can also provide some of the most evocative
photography opportunities in Cairo. Unlike many mosques, it
is rarely busy, and one is able to wander freely almost every-
where. When I wax lyrical about Ibn Tulun to Egyptian friends,
I am often surprised to find they have never been to it. Then
I remind myself that there are many places in London I have
never been to either. It's easy to forget the most remarkable
things on your doorstep or put them off for another day.

From the steps of the Ibn Tulun minaret you can see the modern
skyline and Islamic heritage of this medieval quarter

Ibn Tulun has its own simple strength

The Blue Mosque also has a central garden, bringing more relief from the overhead sun

The cool and colorful interior of the Blue Mosque (the mosque of Aqsunqur) is unusual for its highly decorative blue-tile work

FOLLOWING PAGES:
These tiles were brought by Ibrahim Agha from either Istanbul or Damascus in the 17th Century

A very different mosque experience is the Blue Mosque (the mosque of Aqsunqur), which is a little off the beaten track on Bab al-Wazir Street, but well worth the walk if you have extra time. There is no guarantee you will get inside, but if you do, a garden of delights awaits. The mosque has recently been restored and now provides a historical visit to many styles of decoration in one place.

This mosque dates from the mid-fourteenth century, although its key attraction, the blue tiles from which it derives its popular name, only arrived in 1652 and must have been a transformative new decorative style for the faithful. These vivid Ottoman tiles provide a wall of vibrant color, which in combination with the courtyard garden make for a very agreeable space to stop. For those who wish to delve further into the history of this mosque and its builders, another tale of nasty intrigue awaits.

al-Azhar Park has been a huge success in terms of providing a green public space for Cairo denizens while bringing fresh beauty to Islamic Cairo

If, after so much wandering among busy and cramped streets, you seek some refreshment and fresher air, nearby al-Azhar Park is a good choice.

Al-Azhar Park is a miracle of modern Cairo. It lies just outside the eastern limit of medieval Cairo, squeezed alongside the busy motorway that is Salah Salem Street. Despite these cramped surroundings and the need to remove five hundred years' worth of garbage from a huge area, the project, funded by the Aga Khan Foundation for Culture to the tune of some US$30 million, created an oasis covering thirty hectares. The park provides much-needed green space for Cairenes and has been cherished ever since it opened in 2005.

The restaurants, pavilions, and seating areas in the park provide wonderful views across Islamic Cairo and the city in all directions. The Moorish style of the buildings and courtyard are something of an Arabian Nights fantasy, especially if you gaze toward the Citadel some miles away. Many things come to mind as you stand and absorb the vista, but for me the message is one of hope. Al-Azhar Park is proof that with determination, cooperation, and vision anything can be turned around.

The inside out perspective from al-Azhar Park's
restaurant area displays the gardens' geometric design

On the far side of Salah Salem Street is the Northern Cemetery of the City of the Dead.

It would be untrue to say that this area remains as easy to visit as it was when I first ventured here in the 1980s. This very much alive city of the dead has become overcrowded, and the older and most interesting monuments have grown less accessible in recent years. For the persistent traveler, however, it can be a rewarding day.

The mausoleum of Ibn Barquq is a beautifully tranquil spot in the midst of the hubbub, and provides some inspirational light for photography. With the correct style of persuasion, it may be possible to climb the minarets and explore the less public areas of this fine, symmetrical building, which was built in 1400 by Farag, the son of Sultan Barquq, in honor of his father. Its inception in what was then desert was also an attempt to create a new community with this building at its heart. The building has been a source of succor to succeeding generations of users.

The glassblower in the City of the Dead endures all-day heat but creates objects of clear distinction

The light and colors of the Ibn Barquq mausoleum mosque are like an orchestra playing in your eyes

When looking into the courtyard one should remember that when first built this tranquil space lay in empty desert

A beautifully inscribed mosque lamp

Out of the sun the carpets show the correct direction of prayer

The keeper of the mosque walks slowly around his territory

The Citadel is one of the most visited and photographed places in all of Cairo

All through this trip around Cairo's historic heart, one feature will have been a constant in the corner of your eye. The Citadel that sits high above Cairo is the former impenetrable fortress of Saladin, who founded this garrison town after his arrival in 1168.

Cairo, and indeed the whole of Egypt, was ruled from here for the next seven centuries under various rulers. It was only some 170 years ago, however, that the mosque of Muhammad Ali, which has become one of Cairo's most iconic symbols, was built. The mosque of Muhammad Ali is, for many, the Citadel proper.

Its imitation Ottoman style represents a key moment in the return of Egypt as a regional leader during that period of Turkish dominance.

Standing at the wall and looking west across the whole of modern Cairo as far as the Pyramids of Giza is a sight to which no photograph can do justice. It is a massive panorama. From inside the mosque itself, or from the courtyards and seating areas, every view is spectacular. The city below, especially the older and Islamic areas, still have a sense of age that transports you.

This fine view shows why the Citadel was built on this spot
with all of Cairo beneath its watchful gaze

Higher still is the simplest possible café, perched by a road on the side of the Muqattam Hills

The inspiring cave churches of Muqattam are a less visited site high above Cairo

Be prepared to be investigated and mobbed by the lovely children who run freely around these churches

This space is like a rock stadium but it's a rock church

Dug from the very rock by a poor but determined community, these spaces look up to the sky in hope

The Muqattam hills are not on the usual list of visitor destinations, although they provide some of the best views of Cairo. Up on the top of Muqattam is a district existing above the worst of the city's pollution. Along the edge is a series of lookout cafés, which are as basic as the coffee they serve. The view, however, is compensation beyond words.

If you have an interest in architecture and an appreciation for hard work, a visit to the cave churches of Muqattam will be among the most uplifting moments of any day out.

Relatively recently, members of the Christian community who live in the area and are mostly responsible for sorting and recycling the city's garbage have dug seven churches from the rock of the hills. These vast amphitheaters are places of worship and community that serve up to twenty thousand churchgoers. The welcome given to visitors is genuinely heartwarming.

As places creating an inside out experience, the churches have no rival for shape, size, light, or context. The very fact of their creation in adverse conditions by a poor but determined group of people makes for a special and inspiring story.

Khan al-Khalili

The view over the rooftops of this old part of the city includes al-Azhar Mosque (left) and the Qalawun complex (above)

The famous labyrinthine market area of Khan al-Khalili, which is the shopping destination for all tourists and many Egyptians, abuts the great market street of Muski; together they comprise an area where you will find anything but the truth.

This is a place to be single-minded if you wish to find and buy a desired item at a price you like. Equally, it can just be a place in which to wander, take photographs, and enjoy a coffee or honey-filled *fiteer* (sweet flaky pastry) at the inaccurately named Egyptian Pancakes restaurant, but the thickness of one's skin is tested by the constant harassment of salespeople. You must take the experience with a smile.

One thing on which everyone seems to agree is that the Khan al-Khalili is named after Jaharkas al-Khalili, an emir of the Mamluk period, who was active around 1382. It was also known as the Turkish Bazaar.

It's easy to imagine the centuries of stories that underpin the place we see today. Families who have traded here for years and have seen everything are effectively battle-hardened. They bargain with equal measures of charm and steel.

If you are prepared to wander boldly, it is an ideal space to enjoy different views and to find unusual perspectives. The main streets are strewn with tourist items of variable quality and even more variable prices, but venture farther inside and high-quality gems can be found. Remember that, with shopping as with many other things, beauty is entirely in the eye of the beholder, and nowhere more so than in the Khan.

From the Hussein Hotel breakfast room you can view al-Azhar Mosque, which every Friday draws thousands of worshipers

Mu'izz Street's buildings are still and quiet while outside the constant flow of hooting traffic navigates these narrow old roads

My only tip when you're tempted to buy is to hold whatever has taken your fancy for thirty seconds and examine it properly. This allows time to consider your choice and tends to scare the salesperson into reducing the price without your actually having to speak.

If you have more time and are able to wander around, then try to look beyond the obvious. Much of what you see has been imported from China in recent years, but there is a drive to return to locally made goods. Above ground level there are hundreds of rooms and workshops, which are the back offices to the Khan al-Khalili. Historically, these places were grouped by type of merchandise in areas called *wikala*s, which still exist today.

Also above ground are hotels for leisure and local business visitors on a budget. They overlook a large square and the mosque of Sayidna al-Hussein. This is a highly venerated place and one of the few mosques that do not encourage non-Muslim visitors. Friday prayers take place in the square outside, and these can be observed without entering the mosque.

From the hotels that sit atop the buildings around the square are some excellent views and photographic opportunities. One aspect of Cairo that surprises many long-term or returning visitors is the great variation in weather over a year. This can make for greatly differing moods and light effects, even when you may have taken a photograph from the same vantage point many times. Always have some kind of camera with you.

The mausoleum and madrasa of Qalawun,
which lie on Mu'izz Street, have been preserved
for new generations of visitors

Avoid the middle of the day and wander the backstreets when the slanted light brings magic to Khan al-Khalili

Fishawi café is that rare example of a tourist trap that does not disappoint

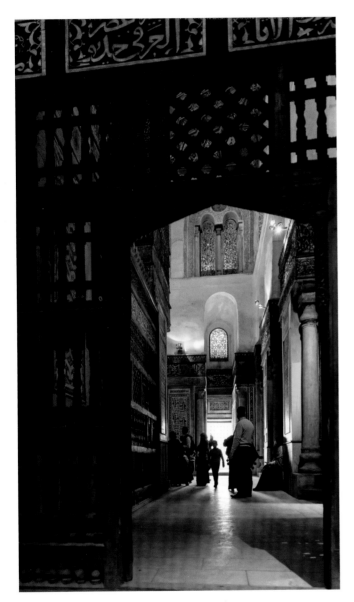

No visit to this area is complete without taking tea or coffee while the world of commerce comes to you. Fishawi café is a special place to do that, lying as it does close to Hussein Square, Khan al-Khalili, and Midaq Alley (famously featured in the novel of the same name by Naguib Mahfouz). The role of Fishawi and its success is based around catering for tourists and locals alike, as well as appealing to all ages. Given that the café claims to have been open twenty-four hours a day for the past two hundred years, it must be succeeding in this balancing act!

Adjacent to the Khan al-Khalili is the impressively renovated Mu'izz li-Din Illah Street, where, in just a few hundred meters, you can visit almost every building and be transported to the exotic East, as imagined in the *Arabian Nights*. The interiors offer a sense of otherworldliness that fits the Hollywood portrayal of the magical East.

These majestic interiors all look out at some point onto modern-day Cairo through the windows and *mashrabiya* (carved wood latticework) screens. In some cases the light floods from above onto courtyards, or streams in through colored glass. I find this quiet, assured sense of historic space, so close to the real world just feet away, a marvelous crossing point from the imagined past to the less attractive reality that engulfs you as you head home.

As you wander the buildings of Mu'izz Street consider the wonderful decorative aspects of these great spaces

These spaces provide a respite from
a hard day's work or walking

OPPOSITE:
The Hammam of Sultan Inal is an
elegantly kept memory of the glory days
of bathing in Khan al-Khalili

PRECEDING PAGES:
Mausoleum of the Qalawun complex

Old Cairo to Maadi

It seems almost unfair for one city to have such a depth of historical treasures within its walls, but Cairo has been blessed with concentrated areas of astounding historical importance.

Thus, within a few minutes' stroll of each other are several of the earliest and most beautiful churches, as well as Egypt's oldest synagogue.

The Hanging Church, the Church of Saint George, the Church of Saints Sergius and Bacchus, and the Church of Saint Barbara are all focal points in the history of the Coptic Church and, while they have all undergone renovation over the centuries, the sense of being in a truly old place of real importance is palpable.

What is termed Old Cairo is defined by the ancient city walls known as Babylon, which served as the Roman fortress in the third century AD and is likely to have been the place where the Holy Family found sanctuary during their flight to Egypt. There are many sites associated with this visit scattered along the Nile. The family passed through Qantara, the Delta, and Heliopolis before finding safety from Herod's reach in what is now an important area in Christian heritage and history.

At the time of their arrival, this tight, narrow-walled community was something of a forgotten enclave, as it was in Alexandria that culture and art thrived under Greek influence. The large Jewish community that lived in Babylon is still celebrated here, as evidenced by the beautiful, recently renovated synagogue of Ben Ezra, which is surrounded by the churches of early Coptic Egypt.

The narrow winding streets of Old Cairo have a natural sense of being both indoors and outside. OPPOSITE: Windows in the Church of Saint George.

The Biblical stories that underpin the history of Old Cairo's importance are mirrored in the vast array of paintings and artifacts that fill every corner of the churches and play a key part in the daily devotional life of the very active Coptic population, which now numbers over ten million across Egypt.

A visit to the religious buildings in the area is always a heartwarming experience. The welcome you receive is genuine and any curiosity or interest in the history of the area is appreciated. Apart from visiting the churches themselves, wandering the labyrinthine streets is an opportunity to enjoy another great historical time shift.

The photographs here capture mere glimpses of the great range of light and shade these buildings create at varying times of day. Emerging from the relative gloom to the light outside or finding a vantage point to look out across the magnificent diversity of buildings and towers, cemeteries, and the Coptic Museum offer a real opportunity to savor the past.

The dome of Saint George is naturally illuminated

These historically rich streets have seen Jewish, Christian, and Muslim communities who lived side by side in shared spaces

Leaving the Hanging Church and its ancient history you are struck by the encroachment of new buildings

Just a short journey away, on Roda Island, is one of Cairo's greatest yet least visited treasures: Manial Palace.

If you wish to experience royal history and get a feel for the Ottoman-era glories of late-nineteenth-century Cairo, a long, leisurely visit to Manial Palace and Museum is a treat for the eyes and soul.

The huge walled area contains several buildings connected by pathways through a fine collection of trees and plants, which provide quiet corners to sit and rest between the various highlights of your walk around the complex. Any time of day is a delight.

The palace was built by Prince Muhammad Ali Tawfiq in the early part of the twentieth century, and is a somewhat crazy mix of interior styles that shout opulence at every turn. As you wander from room to room, it is easy to imagine the conversations, social whirl, intrigue, and glamour of the incidents that occurred within the walls of the palace itself and carried great influence beyond them.

The prince was the uncle of King Farouk as well as his chief regent, and the son of Khedive Tawfiq I. As such, for much of his life he was the heir presumptive of Egypt and Sudan, until the birth of King Farouk's son, Ahmad Fouad. Soon after this,

The foyer of the Manial Palace draws on Turkish
and Moorish influences while the house as a whole
includes inspiration from Morocco to Persia

The ceiling of the main hall of Manial
Palace allows a cool light to illuminate
every detail of its decorative styles

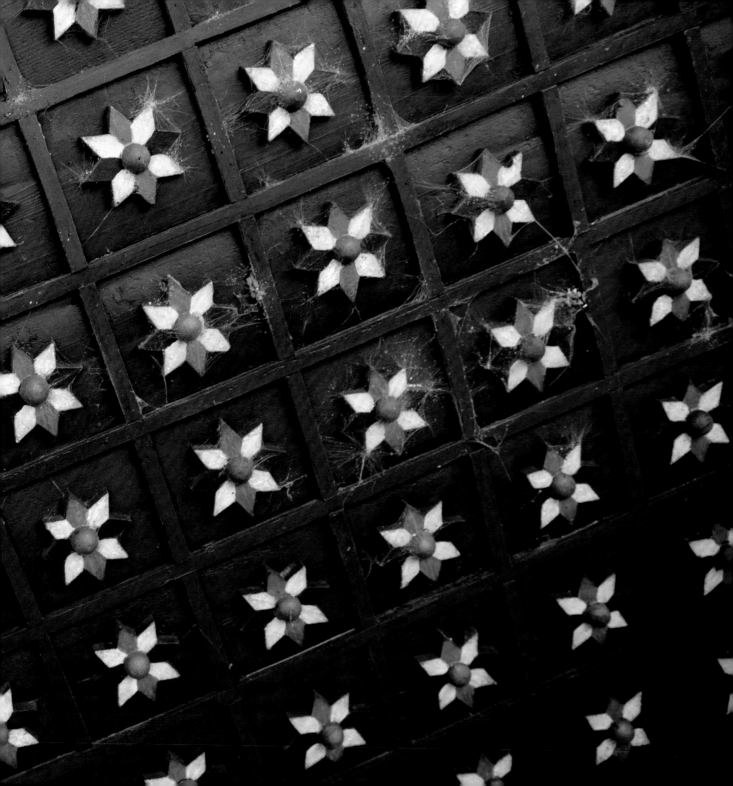

The mosque in Manial Palace is
a masterpiece of Islamic style, and one of
the most ornate spaces in the complex

PRECEDING PAGES:
Intricate details adorn every surface
of the Manial Palace interiors

The hunting lodge museum

These formal meeting rooms have an air of sophisticated officialdom and a fascinating period feel

Egypt was declared a republic and, like many members of the royal family, the prince left for exile in Europe. He died in Lausanne in 1955.

The royal heritage in Manial Palace and its grounds has created one of the few places where one can feel close to that period in Egypt's history. The popularity of King Farouk

has ebbed and flowed in Egypt but fascination with the man and his time has endured, as evidenced by the wide range of visitors to the palace.

We were fortunate enough to photograph the buildings and grounds on a beautiful day soon after they had been restored following ten years of careful workmanship. The gardens, mosque, palace building, and clock tower all underwent decorative and structural work of various kinds, and the results are stunning. The architecture blends the interior styles of the Ottomans, Syrians, North Africans, and Persians—a heady and tantalizing mixture.

From an inside out perspective, these buildings and grounds have it all. Period styles of the highest quality combine with architectural brilliance to keep rooms cool, light, and functional. The textiles, carpets, and furniture that fill the rooms are also of great beauty and interest.

To enjoy the experience to the full you must be prepared. There are no shops in the museum, and around the area very few places sell snacks or food. I recommend taking a picnic and allowing yourself time to linger in the grounds. As you move through the buildings, the changing light and shifts in temperature from hot to cool are apparent, your eyes constantly adjusting to cope. Take time to absorb each building and the spaces within. Sit under a tree, find a bench, read the names of the trees and plants that form the collection and imagine how they came to be in this Cairo palace. Enjoy the solitude and isolation from the street outside the walls and try to imagine what it was like to have been part of one of the richest royal dynasties in the world and to enjoy such opulence and patronage. Read something about them, and perhaps return to sit in the grounds of Manial with a book. It's one of those rare spots where you can do that and be left largely alone.

A ceiling to intimidate the most royal of royal guests

The garden is a relaxed blend of ancient civilizations and a wonderful indoor
retreat from the buildings and traffic outside

Manial Palace has a unique feel, the outcome of changing royal and cultural
influences that makes it a place of fun surprises at every turn

After Cairo's central neighborhoods, Maadi comes as a pleasant suburban surprise

After luxuriating amid the greenery and being able to wander at will, you may wish for more of the same. Heading south to Maadi is a good option. Just a few stops on the Metro line bring you to Road 9 and its many shops and restaurants.

Maadi is a relatively modern part of Cairo, and an area well known for its wider roads, larger villas, and green spaces. It was developed into this modern suburb at the start of the twentieth century, originally planned by a Canadian named Alexander J. Adams immediately after the opening of the railway line from Cairo to Helwan. It grew in size and importance during the Second World War as a base for the large number of soldiers from New Zealand, who chose the area as a rather luxurious home for themselves.

In modern times, it is hard to believe that Maadi had noise-after-dark regulations, as well as rules ensuring all gardens were kept in good order. Although there are still many beautiful gardens, they are often hidden behind walls and trees.

Looking out onto Road 9 you will find people shopping and eating 24 hours a day

Traditional stores such as ironmongers are owned by proprietors who have spent their whole life in the business

Flower shops bring color and life to many street corners

Road 9 has many cool and quiet stores to explore

Road 9 acts as the unofficial downtown of Maadi and, as you can see from these photographs, some of its many stores uphold traditional appearances and services. To rummage around the bric-a-brac is fun, but it's even more relaxing to sit and watch the world go by as these shopkeepers do and, in all likelihood, as their parents did before them.

After spending some time on Road 9, you might wander the streets between it and Road 21 to see some lovely houses and well-maintained squares, and revel in an unusual low-rise green environment. As in all of Egypt, the relentless population growth means a quiet walk is hard to enjoy, but here, at certain times of day, you can walk, jog, and ride a bicycle without the constant fear of an accident.

Newer businessmen take advantage of Maadi's younger,
family-oriented customer base

In the small mini-markets off the main
road are other specialist stores and
interesting denizens

Pyramids and Pharaohs

No one can say they have been to Cairo without making a trip to the Great Pyramid of Giza, but, as with many trips to iconic monuments, a visit can be somewhat underwhelming. Decades of construction and hordes of visitors have virtually destroyed the atmosphere around the site, but with a bit of planning, you can add on some side trips that will make this day out truly memorable.

As you head toward the southern edge of Cairo and finally sense you're leaving the city behind, the concept of inside out changes. The main difference is the never-ending sky once the city's tall buildings and heaving streets are left behind.

Suddenly, the air improves and the horizon opens out.

This happens closest to Cairo at what is one of Egypt's most popular tourist offerings, set on an island south of the city. It took me some thirty years to visit Dr. Hassan Ragab's Pharaonic Village because I had wrongly assumed it would be a terrible experience. The village itself was a natural development of the work of Dr. Ragab, who, having devoted himself to redeveloping the art of papyrus making, founded the Papyrus Institute on Jacob Island in 1968, which later became the Pharaonic Village. He planted five thousand trees on the island to create this special spot.

For those fortunate enough to have been to Luxor and know its special atmosphere, the Pharaonic Village has the same feeling of timelessness, in keeping with the village's efforts to take you back over three thousand years. As you glide around on open barges, the foliage, water, and wildlife all ensure you lose any sense of being in Cairo and transport you for an hour or two. Here, as in many places in Egypt, if

Ancient glassblowing techniques as seen looking out from the boat which carries you around the island of the Pharaonic Village (opposite)

you close your eyes and then reopen them, you can feel you have traveled back in time. I had thought that the village would be a tourist trap, but in fact it is enjoyed mainly by Egyptians of all ages. Watching people rediscover their own history is delightful.

It is educational to see how crafts such as glassblowing and weaving were developed to such a high standard, and how farming has barely changed over the millennia. The recreated temple may not look very old, but the quality of information the guide gave inside was excellent and amusing.

Jacob Island's timeless aura has been encroached
on by the relentless building around it

The reception area of the Pharaonic Village
has a lovely closeness to the river

Leaving the village, you may choose to head toward the edge of town and face one of Egypt's great challenges: how to actually see the Pyramids of Giza without being hassled, and how to contemplate their enduring beauty and magnificence in peace. It is not easy.

Photographically and physically, I suggest an outside-in approach at Giza. The best views, if you wish to understand the sheer scale and setting of the last remaining Wonder of the Ancient World, are from the very edge of the site. Indeed, in some cases, it is best to be outside altogether.

The best full-frontal view of the Pyramids and the Sphinx can be observed through the upper windows and roof of the Pizza Hut opposite the main entrance to the Giza site. This jarring juxtaposition of past and present is in itself highly entertaining, and if you go there after visiting the site itself, it will feel relatively peaceful and much more relaxing. This is a view that really cannot be replicated anywhere in the world. The sense of uniqueness in time and place is one to carry away and store in your memories.

Outside the main entrance near the Sphinx are streets that assault the senses, especially if you appear to be any kind of tourist. All manner of goods and services, from papyrus to camel rides, are thrust at you, so that finding some kind of refuge becomes imperative.

One excellent option is the bookstore that faces the Pyramids and Sphinx. After the experience of the Pyramids up close, you may wish to read more or buy pictures that reflect your visit. The store is cool, and the light filtered through the doors is relaxing and encourages browsing and sitting in the chairs provided. The photograph on the right shows a view from the door, which encompasses thousands of years of time travel. The bookstore interior leads out to a busy street of young Egyptians, horses, and carts, and beyond them the face of the Sphinx and the pyramid of Khafre.

The Pyramids are physically tough to engage with—after all, they were designed for the dead rather than the living. While it is possible to go inside the Pyramids at Giza, you would be lucky to have them to yourself, and in all likelihood you will be one of many inside a suffocating space. This experience is certainly not for those suffering from claustrophobia. By far the best overview of the Giza pyramid site is from the desert. This can mean a camel ride, and I would urge you to do that, even if it seems a typically touristy thing to do. Negotiate hard, and then relax once you are aboard. The image of the Pyramids so close to the vastness of Cairo beyond will stay in your mind forever.

Many ages run together in parallel when you are near the Pyramids

At Saqqara, Pharaoh Zoser looks out from
a stone box on the world outside

The restaurants around the Saqqara site
are built of cloth and rope

They offer a simple homely style and wonderful food

Some thirty minutes away are two of the best archaeological sites in Egypt. Both provide the chance to escape and appreciate the landscape and special nature of Egypt's fertile land.

Saqqara and Dahshur, the two largest sites after Giza, include pyramids and tombs to explore, but also allow one to appreciate how the culture of the Old Kingdom grew around these extraordinary first forms of stone architecture around the Third Dynasty (Old Kingdom) during the reign of Zoser (2667–2648 BC). During his time, Egypt enjoyed a period of peace and stability, and supporting Zoser was one the Egypt's most influential figures—a man named Imhotep.

Imhotep was a trusted vizier, a judge, and a high priest, among many other important roles. He came to occupy such a special position as a demigod that his legacy endured throughout pharaonic history.

It was Imhotep who had the vision to take a *mastaba* (tomb) and build upward in levels of decreasing size. Thus were the pyramids born, and the fact that the Step Pyramid of Saqqara is still here to visit and marvel at over five thousand years later is testament to his skill and to that of thousands of workers.

Saqqara offers many remarkable viewpoints. Whether you look north or south, you see pyramids. Saqqara is a fascinating site to wander around and should be taken at one's own pace before taking a break at one of the lovely outdoor restaurants that border the road leading to it.

For many, this excursion may well be their first encounter with the real farmland and village life of Egypt. Looking out from a vehicle at the bright sun and intense green of the fields, it is easy to see how little some aspects of Egyptian life have changed.

Looking south from Saqqara along the pyramid field, you may be surprised to see two very large pyramids in the distance. The Bent Pyramid and the Red Pyramid would be highlights of most countries' tourist sites for sheer size and historical interest, but in Egypt they are just a little too far from the city for the majority of short-stay visitors to reach.

In the fields around Saqqara buildings await use by people and animals for the shade they provide

This makes them ideal, of course.

One of the main reasons Dahshur and its delights are so sparsely enjoyed is that the recent history of this site included years when it fell inside a military area and was closed to public access. Over those years, an out-of-sight, out-of-mind sensibility prevailed and the pyramids were forgotten for and by tourists. This situation, combined with their relative distance from the city, created the semi-isolation that can be enjoyed now.

The so-called Bent Pyramid is a marvel of shape survival. How did it get built and how has it remained standing? These are the questions that come to mind when you see this odd structure for the first time. With much of its casing still intact, it is at once well preserved and incomplete.

Standing above the edge of the desert by the fertile farmland of the Nile Valley, it is a testament to bad mathematics. This is probably a harsh judgment, however, on what is thought to be the pharaohs' first attempt at a true pyramid, built on the orders of Sneferu in around 2600 BC.

Sneferu was the father of Khufu, builder of the Great Pyramid at Giza.

The inside of the Red Pyramid is dramatically lit and a fun place in which to let your imagination run wild

Leaving from the inside to the light beyond always comes as a (literal) breath of fresh air

The Bent Pyramid is incomplete in that it was never used for its intended purpose. When it became clear that the angle of building was impossible to maintain from the base to the summit, the pyramid was topped out at a lower angle. Its abandonment (a sense of which prevails even today) is to my mind the very essence of its charm. Visit in the cooler times of year and you may have the site all to yourself. Picnic there and walk around at ease. There is a smaller, collapsed, pyramid nearby that one may climb if it is quiet. It is also a terrific place to take photographs. However, you cannot go inside. After watching his first pyramid go horribly wrong, the pharaoh ordered another one for his eventual entombment to be built nearby. The

Looking out from the parking area to the Bent Pyramid is exciting for any visitors as they arrive

so-called Red Pyramid, which can claim to be the first successfully completed true pyramid, can today be visited and entered.

It is hard work but rewarding, and often you will be the only person or group in the chamber itself, which, despite a pungent odor, is a large and fascinating space in which to understand the internal structure of these very early pyramids.

Looking up the ramp that takes you from below ground to the exit high above is a unique experience. Picture the workers or the pharaoh's senior figures doing just this some five thousand years ago. You can imagine the sense of relief they felt when they emerged and looked across an Egypt empty of today's cities and roads, and perhaps in annual flood.

The craftspeople and weavers of the Wissa Wassef Center work in cool and naturally lit adobe-style buildings

Light fall on the tapestries

Having made the trip to this area, a visit to the Ramses Wissa Wassef Art Center is a must. This museum, gallery, and shop have been producing tapestry weavings by Egyptian villagers for over sixty years at Harraniya near Giza. Set in beautiful gardens and traditional adobe buildings, the center is a model business, combining a strong ethical code based on equality and opportunity for all with commercial and artistic values that strive for the highest possible standards. Created under the guidance of the Wissa Wassef family for two generations, the best of this remarkable woven folk art can be seen in venues such as the Victoria and Albert Museum and the British Museum, among others. Here you may wander and see people of all ages weaving or learning the art for a new generation.

As a sensory experience, the gardens are a slice of paradise and the store is hard to resist. The architecture of the buildings blends perfectly with the surroundings, and the light and shade combine with the natural movement of air to create a permanent cool spot.

Traditional architectural style
with an artistic touch

The Wissa Wassef gallery area uses natural light from above and the door to illuminate this subtly colored work

Depending on your budget, Pizza Hut (above) or the Mena House Hotel
(opposite) offer very different experiences but both deliver amazing views

OPPOSITE: Beautifully changing views created
by the sun's daily path can be observed from the
Mena House restaurant's sensational interior

It seems logical to end this book with a classic view from a special place. The pure enjoyment felt when looking out from the Mena House Hotel at any time is unique in world travel. This famous place has true Grand Hotel heritage and started life as a hunting lodge built by Khedive Ismail before being used as a resthouse for the Empress Eugenie. After she opened the Suez Canal and left, it became a hotel that has since hosted every famous politician and celebrity imaginable. The views from the restaurant or bar in the original building are breathtaking and represent the perfect version of Cairo inside out. Every era is in view, from ancient Egypt to the modern day, with colonial grandeur all around.

The sense of time travel and glamor are quite delicious and the interior itself a museum of quality design. The pool area and gardens also provide a welcome quiet place to escape the tourist hassle just beyond the hotel's gate. Egypt has much to offer and in some places retains its history with style and aplomb. The Mena House has all this and more and is well worth the journey.

Few bars in the
world can compete
with this inside-out
panorama at the
Mena House

The scene from the Mena House pool with both ancient and modern styles to admire seems a fitting end to this book